Rhinos

Patricia Kendell

HODDER
Wayland

An imprint of Hodder Children's Books

Alligators Chimpanzees Dolphins Elephants
Giraffes Gorillas Grizzly Bears Hippos
Leopards Lions Orangutans Pandas Penguins
Polar Bears Rhinos Sea Otters Sharks Tigers

 © 2003 White-Thomson Publishing Ltd

Produced for Hodder Wayland by White-Thomson Publishing Ltd

Editor: Kay Barnham
Designer: Tim Mayer
Consultant: Stuart Chapman – Head of WWF-UK's Endangered
   Species Programme
Language Consultant: Norah Granger – Senior Lecturer in Primary
   Education at the University of Brighton
Picture research: Shelley Noronha – Glass Onion Pictures

Published in Great Britain in 2003 by Hodder Wayland,
an imprint of Hodder Children's Books.

Photograph acknowledgements:
Bruce Coleman 26 (Trevor Barrett), 15 (Jane Burton),
8 (Natural Selection Inc); FLPA 27 (Foto Natura Stock),
16 (F Hartmann), 4, 9 & 32, 18 (David Hosking),
12 (Gerard Lacz), 22 (Minden Pictures), 20 (Silvestris),
6, 19 (Terry Whittaker), 13, 14 (Martin B Whithers);
NHPA 11 (Silvestris Fotoservice), 10 (Stephen Kraseman);
OSF 5, 21 (Mike Birkhead), 25 (Deni Brown),
29 (Stan Osolinski); Still Pictures 24 (Mark Edwards),
17 (Fritz Polking), 7, 23, 28 (Roland Seitre).

British Library Cataloguing in Publication Data
Kendell, Patricia
   Rhino. – (In the wild)
   1. Rhinoceros (Genus) – Juvenile literature
   I. Title II. Barnham, Kay
   599.6'68

ISBN: 0 7502 4233 7

Printed and bound in Hong Kong

Hodder Children's Books
A division of Hodder Headline Limited
338 Euston Road, London NW1 3BH

Produced in association with WWF-UK.
WWF-UK registered charity number 1081247.
A company limited by guarantee number 4016725.
Panda device © 1986 WWF ® WWF registered trademark owner.

Contents

Where rhinos live

There are two types of **rhinoceros** that live in Africa. The white rhino lives in grasslands.

The black rhino lives in **scrubland**.
Other members of the rhino family
live mainly in forests in parts of Asia.

Baby rhinos

Most rhinos have only one **calf** at a time.
Baby rhinos can stand up on their own
just an hour after they are born.

The calf will drink milk from its mother
for about 12 months. It will also start to eat
other food when it is about one week old.

Looking after the calf

A calf will stay close to its mother until she has another calf, usually when the first calf is about two or three years old.

A female rhino will stand guard over her
calf if she senses danger. When it is safe,
she lets the calf run ahead of her.

9

Family life

Mothers and their calves often stay together
in small groups.

Male rhinos usually live alone in a **territory**.
They will fight other males to keep them away.

Growing up

A calf learns all it needs to know about what to eat and where to find water from its mother.

Young male rhinos play-fight with older rhinos.
This teaches them how to **defend** themselves.

Eating...

Rhinos eat only plant food. The big, wide mouth of the white rhino helps it to eat a lot of short grass quite quickly.

Other rhinos have a **flexible** top lip, a bit like the end of an elephant's trunk. This helps them to grasp and eat woody plants.

...and drinking

Most rhinos drink from a waterhole every
day, usually at dusk when it is cooler.

Sometimes they have to walk a long way
to find a new waterhole.

Keeping cool

When it is very hot, a rhino will find
a shady place to rest.

Some rhinos enjoy **wallowing** in cool, muddy water. This also protects them against insect bites.

Keeping in touch

Rhinos have very poor eyesight. They **recognise** one another mainly by smell.

They can turn their ears to pick up sounds.
This helps them to find other rhinos and
also keep out of danger.

On the move

Rhinos can charge at high speed, roaring loudly. They have been known to attack and overturn cars and trucks.

Sometimes rhinos charge when they are
frightened. As they cannot see clearly,
it seems safer to take action! But, most
of the time, they are peaceful animals.

Threats...

Many rhinos do not have enough space
to live in because people are taking
more of their territory to grow food.

Roads and towns divide up the rhinos' territory. This can make it difficult for a male rhino to find a **mate**.

...and dangers

Poachers kill rhinos for their horns, which are made into medicine.

People will pay a lot of money for rhino horn medicine, which is used to cure fevers.

Helping rhinos to survive

Laws have been made to stop people selling
rhino horn. This **park ranger** is making sure
that poachers do not attack the rhinos.

Special protected areas are the best hope for rhinos in the future. Here, they have enough space and are safe from harm.

29

Further information

Find out more about how we can help rhinos in the future.

ORGANIZATIONS TO CONTACT

WWF-UK
Panda House, Weyside Park,
Godalming, Surrey GU7 1XR
Tel: 01483 426444
http://www.wwf.org.uk

International Rhino Foundation
c/o The Wilds
14000 International Road
Cumberland
OH 43732
USA
http://www.rhinos-irf.org

BOOKS

Black Rhino (Animals in Danger): Rod Theodorou, Heinemann Library 2001.

Rhinos: Sally M Walker, Carolrhoda Books 1996.

Rhinos (Animals): Kevin J Holmes, Bridgestone Books 2000.

Rhinos – Horn-Faced Chargers (Wild World of Animals): Lola M Schaefer, Capstone Press 2001.

Glossary

WEBSITES

Most young children will need adult help when visiting websites. Those listed have child-friendly pages to bookmark.

http://animal.discovery.com
This website has video film about rhinos.

http://www.thebigzoo.com
Good information about rhinos can be found at this site, along with interesting photos. Children can also hear a rhino eating.

calf – a baby rhino.

defend – to protect from harm.

flexible – very bendy.

mate – male or female partner. They make babies together.

park ranger – people who look after the special places where wild animals are protected.

poachers – people who break the law by hunting, catching or killing animals.

recognise – to know who someone is.

rhinoceros – the proper name for 'rhino'.

scrubland – grassy land with a few small trees and low bushes.

territory – the home area of an animal.

wallowing – rolling in mud.

Index